BREATH OF EDEN

Breath of Eden

Copyright © 2019 by James Kangas

Cover art: Jan van Kessel the Elder (1626-1679), *Vanitas Still Life* (circa 1665/1670), National Gallery of Art. Washington, D.C. Usage rights are in the public domain.

Cover design by Seth Pennington

All rights reserved. No part of this book may be reproduced or republished without written consent from the publisher, except by reviewers who may quote brief excerpts in connection with a review in a newspaper, magazine, or electronic publication; nor may any part of this book be reproduced, stored in a retrieval system, or transmitted in any form, or by any means be recorded without written consent of the publisher.

Sibling Rivalry Press, LLC
PO Box 26147
Little Rock, AR 72221

info@siblingrivalrypress.com

www.siblingrivalrypress.com

ISBN: 978-1-943977-66-6

By special invitation, this title is housed in the Rare Book and Special Collections Vault of the Library of Congress.

First Sibling Rivalry Press Edition, September 2019

BREATH OF EDEN

James Kangas

SIBLING RIVALRY PRESS
DISTURB/ENRAPTURE
Little Rock, Arkansas

The burned and dusty garden said:
"My leaves are echoes, and thy earth
Is packed with footsteps of the dead."

> "An Athenian Garden"
> —Trumbull Stickney

Contents

11	El Niño (1998)
12	At Frost Gardens
13	Fistful of Daffodils
14	Trumpet Piece
15	Mining Town
16	The Museum of Natural History
17	Dazzleblitz Tutorial
18	Insects in the Wind
19	Gardens of Earthly Delights
20	Celestial Parties
21	Luminescence
23	The Moon as Fat Lady
25	Breath of Eden
26	Outsider
27	The Clock
28	Short Take
29	The Allure of Heavenly Bodies
30	Auld Lang Syne
32	Mr. America
33	Driving to Detroit Through Silverdome Traffic with Nothing in Common
34	Remnants of 1977
37	Rosemary
38	Bonefire
39	Trout Creek Cemetery: August Morning
41	Slow Freight
43	A History

El Niño (1998)

Twisters rip through Florida, turning
swaths of palms and homes to kindling.
And rain keeps drenching California
slopes: mud hills flatten,
raging washouts ruin each day's crop
of hope, and Highway 1 slides in the ocean.
Poor saps who prize their golden

geographies! But here, late February,
mild Michigan winter, what little snow...
gone, ruination not the weather's fault,
I hear a cardinal's insistent song:
Will you come and be my mate? Thick
with gorgeous red feathers, he calls and calls.
In every blasted corner of creation

we get stuck to spend our fates down,
yet with some luck, meet with tugs
and beauties to distract us: streets
of glowing, playful, sweet-eyed natives,
land- or dream- or waterscapes, or winning
weather (sometimes gone berserk
to rage like flesh in love). And time

keeps raining down our daily lot
of wanting whatnot, all. A gullied
face which haunts my bathroom mirror now
laughs at every washed-up worldly wish
my heart had, when I had a heart.
Tell me where on earth to lay the blame,
on whom or what? Why not some boy?

At Frost Gardens

The lilies want only titillation:
insects, the wind god, hummingbird
tongues, any intruder to jostle
their filaments. Have eyes ever
seen a galaxy as sensual as this
radiance of waxy, six-pointed stars,
these quivering anthers?
Yet surely it's their fleetingness
that makes us dote and sigh,
name them the most beautiful
sorrows in the world.

Fistful of Daffodils

It is, of course, futile—
their sunniness snapped off
at the ground, stuffed into a white

cylinder in this flopping arrangement;
and their quaint, protuberant,
flared-out lips each mouthing O

in another direction (so many
angles of ruffled O) proclaiming
their shock, their guiltlessness, over

collar-corollas like dogs' ears
flapped back from reproof. How much
can we ask of them standing here?—

corona, perianth on hollow stems—
holding in those paper mouths
their privates like tongues, blurting

out the unmatched yellow mysteries
we crave, saying *Happy to see you*, cut
dead, and just crazy to give.

Trumpet Piece

Ruing his father, in a new school
he shyly raised his open hand
when Mr. Hathaway asked
in class if anyone wanted to learn
the trumpet. It started then
once a week, a half hour
before the morning bell: the boy's
desire from some deep spring, his
nervous sweat, his unspoken worship,
his effort to please his newfound
idol (so golden—in collar, tie,
tweed coat, smelling of after-
shave and sincerity) who taught
the kid with unsuited teeth
an embouchure first, a decent
sound, a C scale, "Abide with Me."

Abide with him? Yes, please. And
with fingers awkward on the mother-
of-pearl that capped the keys, lips
set tight on the cold metal cup
and his twelve-year-old's lungs,
he tooted his best on his tutor's
instrument, the brass (or was it
silver?) tubing, redolent of holy
spit and valve oil, wanting
to feel on his flannel shoulder,
on his back, his neck, that strong
warm palm, to touch this
shining man's heart, to be to him
joy, star pupil, his prized
begotten flesh somehow, his
fanfare, anthem, voluntary.

Mining Town

Two prepubescent boys (well really, Jeffrey, you
had edged towards your body's flux ahead of me)—
a sort of brash, precocious knight and page,
we fought with stick swords in the woods
behind the school, contriving our own legend
in that blueprint, pastel, company town, so new
that ground had not been broken for a boneyard,
and all the houses looked the same, and families
came and went. We were brats on the streets
at Halloween: paraffined windows in our wake;
doorsteps graced with luminaries (flaming paper
bags of dog turds) as we knocked, and ran.
Down by the mud-red river, you pioneered
at being adult. I was dumbstruck when you stuck
your penis into the pulp of a ripe cantaloupe
you'd cut a hole in, going straight to the heart
of the thing as though it were heaven.
You pressed me to try it, but I had to beg off.
It seemed so uninviting, and I was so clearly
the amateur. When out of the blue, my father
quit the mine, I had a month as your chum
to mull the umpteen parts I couldn't comprehend
about the mad, desirous business of the body.
And then the day before we moved, at dawn,
like an omen, you cropped up in my dreams,
a prince I was servant to (it's the image of you
I've still got filed in my brain)—fleshing out
as you were, drenched in sweat from our afternoon
run to the river, grinning as you undid your buttons.

The Museum of Natural History

Scrubbing Saturdays all spring
at the junior high carwash
bought an 8th grade Chicago—one
day on the town, two in the bus.
In the Y lobby, the peerless
paired up till the class tough
and I were assigned a room

on the nineteenth floor. Who
could sleep so high—the leprous
pigeons on the fire escape?
Who could talk to him? Try
as I might, he didn't grunt
one reply, didn't glance at me.
But then, heaven had never

answered me either, all those pleas
to be one of the guys.
Half our afternoon in the Field
Museum, I stood in front of
the naked mummies, one caved-in
child, their skin like parchment
shrink-wrapped to their bones.

What a way to end up—forsaken
by Osiris, stripped, on display.
All night in the room, I thought of
nothing but their lurid fate. That
and Jack Tucker's solid body
on the next bed, the ultimate
dumb god to pray to for favors.

Dazzleblitz Tutorial

It wasn't in a lecture hall one learned
the art that made all the others pale.
It wasn't in a studio gaping at
a canvas of electric blue larkspurs
in vast north or skylight light. It was
night in the student union where
our eyes had met for weeks, and now
he asked me if by chance I had the time
to have coffee with him, and the stars
out the Gothic windows winked *yes,
oh, he's as cute as a puppy, he will
make you happy*, and the gold-blond
oak wainscoting exhaled a whiff of
tung oil as if to approve.   In his
rented room in a rambling Victorian
we had some perfumed herb tea, I think,
cup after cup, and then our clothes
started to come undone and his kisses
were each a torch and then his tongue
was all over me, reaching (could it be?)
into every orifice and I went wild with
ecstasy, wild with (as far as I knew)
love, and then he flashed his suave
conqueror boy's grin and I saw that
I would want always to study the flesh
in full lather—how the nerves... jerk,
how the body can withstand such voltage.

Insects in the Wind

When that mash note cropped up
on my windshield—almost
as though a butterfly had blown
out of a reedy ditch
and splattered a wash of amber
before my eyes (chance
meetings prone to bad drama
as they are)—I couldn't
believe the weight of that paper
heart. I lurched.
How love (its false seed even)
begets love I learned late.

It begat like a mayfly.
If only I'd ripped up the news
there by the bell tower
and everywhere repeatedly squashed
your advances when I ran into you
all spoony and endearing.
But the stubbornest flame leapt.
Sucked into that blaze
flesh and soul, what could save
a fool wisp of tinder? What
wings in a stiff gust
have a clue where they're steering?

Gardens of Earthly Delights

Mahogany throats
sunk in buff-pink blossoms,

these day lilies can't help it
(on their scapes nipple high) how

few hours they have to witch the world,
how, into their bed, I've come to peer.

Sprung up, fleshed out, and buds flung wide
summers back, it was our throng

swayed and preened in the wind
through a brief golden noontime bask

in the sun. It was in the arboretum
I first glimpsed your matchless glow,

stood dumb—as I do in this garden now—
gawking, and aching.

Celestial Parties

In a fluttering, hot crowd, one face
(a tawny blossom) weakens you. Walk
out into the bracing night air.
You know these things never pan out
but you'll go back in anyway.

In the sky, the virgin stays close
to the lion. Nothing happens to her
either. Nothing has in all these years.
A woman in red nears,
claims these beings could offer
the explanation you haven't found.
She offers her cheek.

Why have you never learned
to wean yourself from your beautiful
disinterested gods?
You have been practicing longer
than one should humanly have to.

If they make you hunger
eventually you will starve, they give
so little.
And the nimbuses they leave
keep burning in your brain,
consume you from within.
It's what gods do.

Luminescence

Even now, even in the thick
of dusk, a poppy glows
phosphorescent in the garden.
The kaffir lily in the kitchen
window emits a paler orange

hue, hungers to have so rich
a fire, to *be* her half-wild
idol. Leaning on the sink,
I sip vodka in the dimness
as they beam their come-ons

to the immediate world,
dishes of flesh I think drunk
on phosphorus or radium
seeming almost to vibrate.
So many little lamps glimmer

somewhere tonight: a golden
face off-stage in a night-
blooming fantasy, the tonic
in my glass, a thousand
human flames I've touched

in other rooms, hemispheres
of momentary radiance. Each
light's ghostliness beckons
to me, gleams in one facet
of my compounding eyes

as I stare—as if watching
my very first nature film:
the frames in time-lapse

of a day going by, a flower's
bloom and wilt, a speeded-up

life. The big picture doesn't
come to focus. As the dark
grows purer, moths clamor
for a porch light. Clearly
time for the next illusion.

The Moon as Fat Lady

Her dimpled bulk powdered,
she lifts off the day bed
and climbs into view
raising whispers and gasps,
and from the low, far corner
of the darkened big top
begins her long arc
across its firmament,
the steel wires invisible,
the skinny-lipped crane man
on the dim, smoky side
of the canvas backdrop.
Big Bertha, I swear,
is a twig next to her—
Madonna Luna, the Queen
of Pasta, patron saint
of the dumpling. They think
she levitates. They think
she's inhaled helium.

Tonight her black cape
doesn't hide very much
(a thin slice of flank),
and in the spotlight she glows
lighting up the whole tent.
How they stomp and whistle!
They can't get enough of her.
In two days she won't use
any cover at all, and all out,
full flesh, she'll
set their blood racing.
Not one soul grasps how much
she hates this gig,

and snipped free by some angel,
given motorized wings,
she'd fly off to the hot star
who shines while she sleeps,
the one she's so drawn to
in the next circus.

Breath of Eden

After one adolescent toot
when you came over to sleep it off
in my adolescent bed, my friend,
virgins the two of us, surely, drawn
towards naked worlds we would soon plunge into,

I woke early (if I slept at all)
wanting to touch you, but instead
slipped from the sheets' cocoon to the chair
where your T-shirt and jeans lay strewn, knelt
to bury my face in them and breathe

you in as I'd breathe in the perfume
and pollen from a rose deep
into my lungs and blood. Nothing
since then has intoxicated me
like that flesh-scented garden, your clothes.

Outsider

Just never quite fitting in with that old gang,
nor in class, nor at work, nor
the family rituals (a picnic, a wake),

somehow not born for human company;
never knowing what to say, how to say
the path was stone strewn, or brushed over,

that it wound up wicked slopes, or that
trees were only statues, and birds
too much noise, how flowers meant sneezing,

and the sun made one squint; that gifts
from the very first to the last that one could
think of were finally empty boxes,

that love reeked of hot illusion,
and disappointment (that sad word) always
hovered like an angel; and surely all one had

ever been was an outsider, an observer, a goose
egg (or its shell), a paltry shadow
of a mock-up of a person. Kilroy.

The Clock

She had been hit by a bus
while the gardens of elsewhere
blazed, glorious and frail, filling

passersby with great waves of joy
or folly. How young she had been, maybe
even beautiful. Two wars had then

played out their slaughter
of millions, and now bums wandered
into the library she worked in.

One ruin of a man read the news
upside down as she Garbo-like flaunted
her nonwooden leg to him, flashed

a maroon grin with her smeared lipstick,
her glass eye roaming, magnifier
in hand, her red ratlike wig

hanging askew. She never thought all
was kaput. Or say, she never lost hope
as long as she breathed. The clock

on the wall tried over and over to
cover its face with its hands. It had
taken stock: that sorry scene, life

out the window, its own numbing circles,
and the reading room ghosts always mocking
Ginny Glue and Paint, bemoaning the dust

of their shelved fame, their flesh, all
lost now, a lost world, with nothing,
no possible hand, as consolation.

Short Take

Instead of mucking through the whole 3 score and 10,
I think we ought to be given the option
of living a telescoped version of it, say
a week (of the adult part anyway):

5 minutes of laughs, 40 of dire news;
2 1/2 days asleep, 1 1/2 good screws
with any luck; surely an irksome, inglorious,
turtle-clocked 36 hours of the job curse;

a whiff of rose, some snatch of melody, a glimpse
of moon in the western sky; cramps
3 dawns running, untold spells on the can; and worst—
boredom, fatigue, and to boot, as ballast,

one or more personal miseries specially chosen.
In the end, toast yourself—for whatever reason:
for hapless love, for words you meant to speak,
for having what it took to last the week.

The Allure of Heavenly Bodies

Reach down a glass from the cupboard;
mouth wants a splash of tonic.
Around how many nubs in one's life
has some motion or other grown chronic?

Look—through the March elm's cold bare arms—
at the moon waltzing round this clod
of dirt she's sighed for for eons. Isn't
there always some dizzying god

to dither around, to cluck over, flex
a knee for, crook an elbow? Yes,
and sad life with no hub to orbit, no crux,
no heart's little hanker, no hook.

Auld Lang Syne

A crazy reunion in my dream:
friends from the dizzy orbits
of my world from 20, 25 years ago came,
and with great whoops
and arms flying around necks,
each greeted the chums he'd known
when life was a green light and all
our glands were going berserk. Libby
gone thin with her stair-step troop,
and Polly, our sweet lamb of perpetual
indulgence, rehashed what they thought
they once wanted from men;
and Barney and Estelle wept
in their champagne for the Plaths
and Picassos they hadn't become.
Rex moaned his loveless lot to Jake
the Flake who blinked
a perfect understanding from his blank
page in the grammar of existence.
How quaint we were—all of us
out in some anonymous dream street
where Camilla waltzed numbly, and manic
Mike whirled round the limb of an elm
like an acrobat. Time was a bit muddled
but we all knew every jot of our
who's-done-what—and-where chronicle:
half of it happenstance, doubtless
passages of love, and surely, tawdry
Audrey's catalog of boys. Well
I was so glad to see them, I kissed
the whole crew. I even kissed Neal,

shriveled Hope in her shroud. Then *pouf*
stood a genie, and we were young again,
happy, broke. It was just as I
recalled it: one had virtually nothing
to forgive.

Mr. America

The young body builder in the laundromat
gazes back, his blaring baby
in a wicker basket, his hands busy folding
towels, happy loops that have dried
his black hair, every twist. We have met
like this before, but for the first time

this Monday evening, as I lay down
The Norman Conquest, untangle my spun
rainbow from the 50 cent washer, he drifts
over and asks nonchalantly what I study
(as if he couldn't read), in his arms
his child: banner, trumpet, shield.

Driving to Detroit
Through Silverdome Traffic
with Nothing in Common

Ash-grey October Sunday and I'm dragging you
to some foreign film on our second date
of vast silences, though right now you are saying
something about one team's loss yesterday
or that blue sports car (you can tell them all apart!)
that's cruising us. We're late,
the trees jaundiced, flushed, feverish.

With one eye on the perfect V of your thighs
and one on the sky's first V of southbound geese
I've seen this fall, I keep from gesturing
towards either wonder, listening now
to your few words, the inscrutable bearings
of your brain waves, as I wing my way
through eight directions of old love vignettes

to the improbabilities of our ever flying in formation,
each to each and both at ease, our destination—
nearness. Damn goose honk, game score, speech—
and those aching, embarrassed trees coming
unglued left and right, and nothing one can do.

Remnants of 1977

Naked

Tut came. I went. Gold
and gold leaf I remember.
Scarab. A bar, the hotel,
you, our tongues
excavating.
      Tut tut.
Our masks had come
undone. Everything had.
I wanted to be buried
forever in you. I think
I still do.

Portrait

You had a kid's rambling
gait, shoulders
shrugging to swallow
your neck, turtlish,
uncertain,
      your body's
language a gut-deep
chagrin. I thought
I could be balm to you.
Was I, a little? Was I
ointment, before fly?

Gifts

Long distance affair—
in specimen boxes, poly,
clear, you sent wee
map, stone: fetishes
magnified.
      Leelanau,
a tent, we got lost
in the dunes, I in you.
You burned Ferlinghetti
in the campfire; stars
beamed as sparks shot up.

Desert

We were laughing. Damn my
phone, damn my dalliance
weeks back at that inane
soirée. You shrank
to silent
      mortification.
I just sank. It might
as well have been Egypt
you drove off to. I might
as well have been embalmed,
my pharaoh.

Memento Mori

Tut's back in Chicago
29 years on. Why go?
Coffinette for his viscera?
Crook and flail? I've been flailed
    enough, in my way
eviscerated. The hotel's
defunct. You are... where?
Centuries have passed
and all the gods too. Only
artifacts left. No you.

Rosemary

The faces of the dead are X'd out,
you tell me, in the gourmet club
photograph taped on her fridge—

to keep things straight
in her mind, maybe. Who knew?
San Francisco, the 80s, what a crew,

what dishes lay on her countertops
and tables, feasts everywhere
for our eyes and tongues.

"There's rosemary, that's
for remembrance—pray you, love,
remember." It was in every dish.

And then I tell you my mother's
address book, lying on my table
now, has similar X's or slash marks

through the names of her dead,
those she scratched out before her
strokes took her too. She could

have made Latin crosses, I quip.
We laugh, hang up. A void descends
on me, black, huge with losses.

Bonefire

When I die, have me
sent to the crematory.
I want the fire. I
want my ashes delivered
to you. Do with me
then as you will:
throw me from a cliff
to the thrashing ocean;
let me fall through
your fingers in a
prairie wind; feed me
to your lilac; under-
take some weirdness of
your inimitable devising.
As you will, I say!
May I be granted
this last, small wish.
I'll be for a moment
in your magnificent
hands after all
these years finally,
one thing I always wanted.

Trout Creek Cemetery: August Morning

After he loosened the stone from its straps,
he hoisted it with the truck's tackle
and lowered it onto a dolly, maneuvered
the two wheels over rough ground,
centered the slab (to the centimeter)
on the base he'd wiped and beaded with glue.

Weeds, quack grass, plastic and silk flowers
tufted the gravelly slope, a few trees,
grey and red marble, some wooden crosses.
Even in the cool morning, he was sweating
like a bull, until finally he was done.
He stood for a while and talked about living

in these parts, the glut of whitetails,
his bow hunting, his wife and daughter.
And setting headstones. The scene was of utter
peace: the canoe on the lake on the black
granite with an eagle and cloud suspended
in the sky. Sally had argued for the etching

and an inscription which turned out to read
(after much ado) "Always in our hearts,"
and she, my bent mother and father, and I
bantered with the man for cheer until
he had to go. At last my brother was
hard luck free. He had nowhere to have to be,

no one to irk him. He could fish forever
if he wanted to. We stood there quietly
and I supposed my folks were drifting off
to his suckling days (or their parents nearby
in the same row, or their own turn soon),
and Sally—ruing lost love, or money.

And there in that stone garden with the laden
earth sagging, I kept pondering
the monument man's flesh, his face, how
in my sorry dust even on such a day
sprouted lust up, perennial as wild carrot,
oxeye daisy, common milkweed.

Slow Freight

If it comes like a slow freight train
trundling a hundred 50-ton cars
down the track, a sleeve
of smoke at its back, and a thundering
noise, and the hot dreams of untraveled boys
(their cares small as a flattened penny);

if it comes like that, the grave
irrevocable approach, the groves of sycamores
soaking up its peevish whistle,
the earth's small sopranos mute
as the rumbling grows, each broken recitative
to be taken up again, each aria's rote

intervals trotted out once the air's
stopped trembling; if it comes
blatantly like that, if I've
gotten strapped to the trestle unawares,
ravaged at the rack by some madness,
some obdurate disease (my great

trance world dreams, my small
careers all past tending, this mind a hive
of torpid bees, this heart a remaindered glove
fitting no hand the world ever held out
for it, not even yours,
and threadbare now from thrumming the bars

of its wretched cell); if it comes like that,
if that's what it comes to, then let it
come when I am at least lucid,
let me know the finality of it, forgive
myself all my follies for once, engage my five
senses for a last rush, and as the train nears

the bend down the track, and I begin to feel
weightless, feel my body float away,
let it be night, haze-free as a vacuum,
that in the last moments it might flood back
how randomly beautiful, how transient it all was
in the dim, apt light of the unaccountable stars.

A History

> "Even when I say 'I love you'
> it is tainted with goodbyes"
> —Bernard Spencer

From the very first
it was full-blown autumn,
thudding her apples

in the dust already, exuding
their apple smell,
their sad knowledge

of summer; and the maples
dropping their millions
of papery hands, wrung

from their thin wrists
in a last farewell flutter,
not one left finally to wave

its painted tissues in the sky,
not one lusty blossom
in the landscape, not

a wren, not the pondered blue
eye of one day, one hour.
Not one.

Acknowledgments & Notes

The author most gratefully acknowledges the following magazines in which these pieces first appeared, many in somewhat different versions.

Atlanta Review: "Trumpet Piece"
Bay Windows: "Mr. America"
Chiron Review: "Dazzleblitz Tutorial," "Mining Town," "Rosemary," "Trout Creek Cemetery: August Morning"
The Evergreen Chronicles: "Bonefire"
Farmer's Market: "At Frost Gardens"
Faultline: "Outsider" (published under the title "Rorschach")
Gertrude: "El Niño (1998)"
Merced River Literary Review: "Gardens of Earthly Delights"
New Letters: "Fistful of Daffodils"
The New York Quarterly: "Remnants of 1977"
Oxford Magazine: "Auld Lang Syne"
Pacific Review (San Diego): "The Allure of Heavenly Bodies"
The Panhandler: "The Museum of Natural History"
Poet & Critic: "Short Take" (published under the title "Cut!")
Poets On: Barriers: "Driving to Detroit Through Silverdome Traffic with Nothing in Common"
Stone Country: "A History"
Storm Cellar: "Luminescence"
Tampa Review: "Insects in the Wind"
Webster Review: "Celestial Parties," "The Moon as Fat Lady"
West Branch: "Slow Freight"
The Windless Orchard: "Breath of Eden"
Yemassee: "The Clock"

"Breath of Eden" also appeared in *Between the Cracks: The Daedalus Anthology of Kinky Verse*, G. Dillard, ed. (Daedalus Pub. Co., 1996).

"Breath of Eden," "Dazzleblitz Tutorial," "Mining Town," "Mr America," and "The Museum of Natural History" also appeared in *Assaracus*.

The phrase "hot illusion" in the poem "Outsider" comes from a poem by Edith Södergran, a Swedish-speaking Finn who lived from 1892 to 1923. The poem, "Landet som icke är" ("The Land That Is Not"), was translated by Stina Katchadourian, and printed in *Love & Solitude: Selected Poems, 1916-1923* (Fjord Press, 1981).

The quotation in the 4th stanza of "Rosemary" is from Shakespeare's *Hamlet*.

Never-ending thanks and love to Bryan Borland and Seth Pennington for making this book possible, patiently taking in stride the author's revisions, and attending to the smallest detail; to Benjamin Grossberg who years ago gave me wise, invaluable counsel on a number of these pieces; to Sandra McPherson, wonderful poet, and writing workshop leader extraordinaire; to my parents, friends, editors, and teachers who have had a significant impact on my life and my writing; to various individuals whose spirits haunt certain pieces in this collection; and to the countless poets, alive and dead, who have written exceptional lines that repeatedly take away my breath and leave me stunned.

About the Poet

Born in Chicago, Jim Kangas spent his early years growing roots in the Upper Peninsula of Michigan, later earning degrees in Music History and Literature and Library Science from the University of Michigan. He has worked for over 50 years in both public and academic libraries, as well as playing viola in a regional orchestra for over 40 years. He lives in Flint, Michigan, with a former street cat called Kitty.

About the Press

Sibling Rivalry Press is an independent press based in Little Rock, Arkansas. It is a sponsored project of Fractured Atlas, a nonprofit arts service organization. Contributions to support the operations of Sibling Rivalry Press are tax-deductible to the extent permitted by law, and your donations will directly assist in the publication of work that disturbs and enraptures. To contribute to the publication of more books like this one, please visit our website and click *donate*.

Sibling Rivalry Press gratefully acknowledges the following donors, without whom this book would not be possible:

- Tony Taylor
- Mollie Lacy
- Karline Tierney
- Maureen Seaton
- Travis Lau
- Michael Broder & Indolent Books
- Robert Petersen
- Jennifer Armour
- Alana Smoot
- Paul Romero
- Julie R. Enszer
- Clayton Blackstock
- Tess Wilmans-Higgins & Jeff Higgins
- Sarah Browning
- Tina Bradley
- Kai Coggin
- Queer Arts Arkansas
- Jim Cory
- Craig Cotter
- Hugh Tipping
- Mark Ward
- Russell Bunge
- Joe Pan & Brooklyn Arts Press
- Carl Lavigne
- Karen Hayes
- J. Andrew Goodman
- Diane Greene
- W. Stephen Breedlove
- Ed Madden
- Rob Jacques
- Erik Schuckers
- Sugar le Fae
- John Bateman
- Elizabeth Ahl
- Risa Denenberg
- Ron Mohring & Seven Kitchens Press
- Guy Choate & Argenta Reading Series
- Guy Traiber
- Don Cellini
- John Bateman
- Gustavo Hernandez
- Anonymous (12)

www.ingramcontent.com/pod-product-compliance
Lightning Source LLC
Chambersburg PA
CBHW051704040426
42446CB00009B/1299